DINOSAUR WORLD

Strange Lizard

The Adventure of Allosaurus

Written by Michael Dahl

Illustrated by Garry Nichols

Special thanks to our advisers for their expertise:

Philip J. Currie, Curator of Dinosaurs,
Royal Tyrrell Museum of Palaeontology, Drumheller, Alberta, Canada

Susan Kesselring, M.A., Literacy Educator,
Rosemount - Apple Valley - Eagan (Minnesota) School District

PICTURE WINDOW BOOKS
Minneapolis, Minnesota

Managing Editor: Catherine Neitge
Creative Director: Terri Foley
Art Director: Keith Griffin
Editor: Patricia Stockland
Designer: Joe Anderson
Page production: Picture Window Books
The illustrations in this book were prepared digitally.

Picture Window Books
5115 Excelsior Boulevard
Suite 232
Minneapolis, MN 55416
877-845-8392
www.picturewindowbooks.com

Printed in the United States of America.

Library of Congress Cataloging-in-Publication Data
Dahl, Michael.
Strange lizard : the adventure of Allosaurus / written by
Michael Dahl ; illustrated by Garry Nichols.
p. cm. — (Dinosaur world)
Includes bibliographical references and index.
ISBN 1-4048-0937-6 (alk. paper)
1. Allosaurus—Juvenile literature. I. Nichols, Garry, 1958- ill.
II. Title.

QE862.S3D335 2004
567.912—dc22
2004018577

No humans lived during the time of the dinosaurs. No person heard them roar, saw their scales, or felt their feathers.

The giant creatures are gone, but their fossils, or remains, lie hidden in the earth. Dinosaur skulls, skeletons, and eggs have been buried in rock for millions of years.

All around the world, scientists dig up fossils and carefully study them. Bones show how tall the dinosaurs stood. Claws and teeth show how they grabbed and what they ate. Scientists compare fossils with the bodies of living creatures such as birds and reptiles, which are relatives of the dinosaurs. Every year, scientists learn more and more about the giants that have disappeared.

Studying fossils and figuring out how the dinosaurs lived is like putting together the pieces of a puzzle that is millions of years old.

This is what some of those pieces can tell us about the dinosaur known as *Allosaurus* (al-oh-SORE-us).

The sun burned in the western sky. Tree trunks and leaves turned gold in the dusky light. Below the branches of a thick forest, a moving shadow sniffed and snorted.

Streaks of reddish light gleamed on a gigantic, muscular back. *Allosaurus* was stomping along a forest trail, hunting for something to fill its empty belly.

Allosaurus was one of the largest carnivores, or meat-eaters, that lived during the Jurassic period. An adult *Allosaurus* weighed between 2 and 3 tons. It was almost as long as a school bus and could have easily stared into a second-story window.

Allosaurus lifted its head and sniffed at the air. Its keen nostrils caught the scent of blood. Somewhere in the forest a creature was dying. A helpless creature could be dinner for *Allosaurus*.

Allosaurus blinked at the sky. Sunlight was fading. It wanted to eat before night filled the thick forest with darkness.

Scientists have dug up *Allosaurus* skulls with huge, empty eye-sockets. The mighty creature's eyes were probably bigger than oranges, or even grapefruit. Even though *Allosaurus* could see well, scientists believe the meat-eater probably only hunted during the daylight.

Allosaurus passed among the trees, breaking branches. Ferns were crushed beneath its heavy feet.

Allosaurus was large, swift, and strong enough to prey on slow plant-eaters like *Stegosaurus* or *Apatosaurus*. Scientists have even found *Apatosaurus* bones scratched with *Allosaurus* teeth marks.

Along the forest path, *Allosaurus* heard a strange sound. A frightened *Stegosaurus* was stumbling toward the meat-eater. Blood ran from a wound in its side. *Allosaurus* opened its jaws and waited for dinner to come closer.

Stegosaurus saw *Allosaurus* and stopped. It hunched in the middle of the forest trail. The small plant-eater squawked in fear and pain.

Behind the spiked and plated creature, *Allosaurus* saw another larger dinosaur. This was the reason *Stegosaurus* was hurt. At the other end of the trail stood a second meat-eater. *Ceratosaurus!*

Allosaurus competed for food with other fierce carnivores, such as the horned *Ceratosaurus* (suh-RAT-oh-sore-us).

Ceratosaurus roared. It did not want to give up its dinner, not even to the bigger *Allosaurus*.

Allosaurus had arms that looked small compared to its huge body, but they were longer than the arms of a *Tyrannosaurus rex*. The three fingers on each hand were armed with curved 6-inch claws. *Allosaurus's* teeth were also curved. The edges of the teeth had tiny, jagged notches like steak knives.

The two predators drew closer and faced each other.
Their tails whipped back and forth angrily.
Their teeth gleamed. *Allosaurus* darted
forward and slashed a sharp claw at
the horned lizard. *Ceratosaurus*
screamed in pain.

Ceratosaurus rammed into *Allosaurus*'s thick body. *Allosaurus* almost fell over. It used its powerful legs and tail to keep its balance.

Allosaurus was wounded, but it was stronger than *Ceratosaurus*. Once more it lunged at *Ceratosaurus* and ripped a chunk of flesh from its side. *Ceratosaurus* roared. It was finished fighting.

Allosaurus stood on two tall, powerful legs. Each foot ended in four clawed toes, three pointing forward, and one toe pointing back toward its tail. *Allosaurus* usually stood on the three bigger toes when walking and running. This allowed it to move and change directions easily.

Allosaurus turned to eat its dinner. *Stegosaurus* was gone. During the battle between the two hungry predators, the small plant-eater had disappeared!

Allosaurus roared in anger. The hungry hunter bounded into the darkening forest, chasing after the hidden *Stegosaurus*.

Huge predators such as *Allosaurus* could suffer serious, even deadly, damage if they stumbled during a fight or while running. The weight of their massive bones and muscles, combined with their speed, would increase the impact of a fall.

Allosaurus heard a rumble. Something was snorting and snuffling in the dusky forest. *Allosaurus* followed the sound and soon spied its prey through a gap in the trees.

Stegosaurus was wading in a small stream.
The plant-eater was bending down for a drink.

Allosaurus's hearing was probably not well developed.
Some scientists think that *Allosaurus* could only hear very
loud or very low sounds.

Allosaurus pounced on its prey. *Stegosaurus* tried to run, but its feet sank into the soft mud. *Stegosaurus* squawked. The meat-eater's jaws had a firm grip on its long neck.

Allosaurus looked up and roared. The mighty meat-eater finally had its dinner.

Allosaurus: Where ...

Allosaurus fossils have been found in the western United States—Colorado, Utah, and Wyoming. *Allosaurus* fossils may have been recovered from Portugal, Africa, and Australia, though these have not all been confirmed.

... and When

The "Age of Dinosaurs" began 248 million years ago (mya). If we imagine the time from the beginning of the dinosaur age to the present as one day, the Age of Dinosaurs lasted 18 hours—and humans have only been around for 10 minutes!

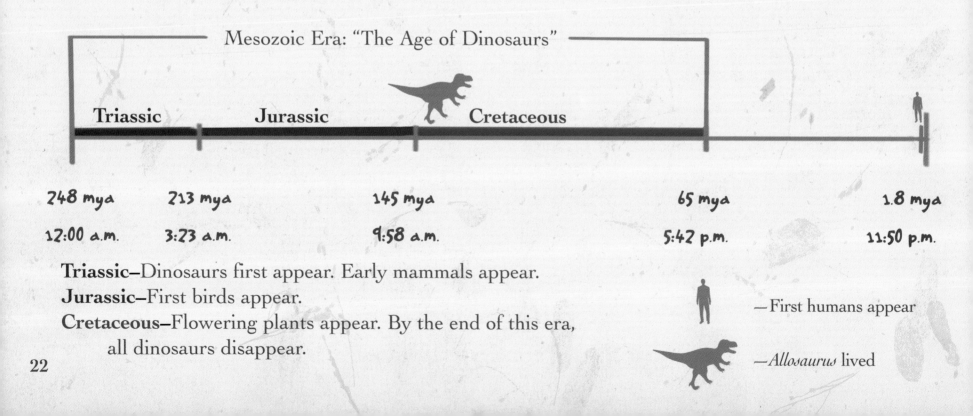

Mesozoic Era: "The Age of Dinosaurs"

Triassic   Jurassic   Cretaceous

248 mya   213 mya   145 mya   65 mya   1.8 mya
12:00 a.m.   3:23 a.m.   9:58 a.m.   5:42 p.m.   11:50 p.m.

Triassic—Dinosaurs first appear. Early mammals appear.
Jurassic—First birds appear.
Cretaceous—Flowering plants appear. By the end of this era, all dinosaurs disappear.

—First humans appear

—*Allosaurus* lived

Digging Deeper

Battle Scars

Life was not easy in the Age of the Dinosaurs, even for a fearsome giant like *Allosaurus*. A skeleton of a young *Allosaurus* dug up in Wyoming shows a creature that suffered lots of bumps and bruises. The skeleton had 14 broken ribs, a broken leg, a broken tail, and infections in its toes and fingers. X-rays show that many of the bones had healed, but the poor dinosaur was probably in pain for most of its life.

Bony Brow

The head of *Allosaurus* was a big bony mass of bumps and ridges. Hard crests, or pointed ridges, over the eyes gave it a different look from other dinosaurs. Some scientists think the ridges provided extra protection to the head, or were used for attracting mates. Other scientists believe the ridges were bony eyebrows, shielding *Allosaurus*'s eyes from bright, tropical sunlight.

Strange Names

Allosaurus was given its name by Othniel Marsh, a scientist who supervised digging teams throughout the western United States in the late 1800s. Marsh's men dug up tons of fossils. When an *Allosaurus* bone was found, it looked different to Marsh from other fossils he had examined. *Allosaurus* means "different" or "strange" lizard. An earlier name for the creature was *Antrodemus*, which means "nightmare dragon."

Big Steps

Allosaurus took big steps. Scientists have discovered footprints left behind by giant *Allosaurus*. A stride is the distance between one print and the next closest print. *Allosaurus*'s stride was 6 1/2 feet (2 meters). The dinosaur's stride was six times the stride of the average adult human!

Words to Know

carnivore—a creature that eats only meat, or other living creatures

dinosaurs—giant creatures that lived millions of years ago; scientists think that many modern reptiles and birds are related to dinosaurs

fossil—the remains of a plant or animal that have hardened into stone

predator—an animal that hunts other animals for food

prey—the animal hunted by a predator

To Learn More

At the Library
Frost, Helen. *Looking At… Allosaurus*. Mankato, Minn.: Pebble Books 2005.

Gray, Susan H. *Allosaurus*. Chanhassen, Minn.: Child's World, 2004.

Wilson, Ron. *Allosaurus*. Vero Beach, Fla.: Rourke Publishing, 2001.

On the Web
FactHound offers a safe, fun way to find Web sites related to this book.
All of the sites on FactHound have been researched by our staff.
www.facthound.com

1. Visit the FactHound home page.
2. Enter a search word related to this book,
   or type in this special code: 1404809376
3. Click on the FETCH IT button.

Your trusty FactHound will fetch
the best Web sites for you!